The Ene

C000253718

Kieran Hu

Based on *An Enemy of the People* by Henrik Ibsen

methuen | drama

LONDON · NEW YORK · OXFORD · NEW DELHI · SYDNEY

METHUEN DRAMA
Bloomsbury Publishing Plc
50 Bedford Square, London, WC1B 3DP, UK
1385 Broadway, New York, NY 10018, USA
29 Earlsfort Terrace, Dublin 2, Ireland

BLOOMSBURY, METHUEN DRAMA and the Methuen Drama logo are
trademarks of Bloomsbury Publishing Plc

First published in Great Britain 2021
Copyright © Kieran Hurley, 2021

Kieran Hurley has asserted his right under the Copyright, Designs
and Patents Act, 1988, to be identified as author of this work.

Cover design: Aglika Hristeva
Cover image © Mihaela Bodlovic

A catalogue record for this book is available from the British Library.

A catalog record for this book is available from the Library of Congress.

ISBN: PB: 978-1-3502-5713-9
ePDF: 978-1-3502-5714-6
eBook: 978-1-3502-5715-3

Series: Modern Plays

Printed and bound in Great Britain

To find out more about our authors and books visit
www.bloomsbury.com and sign up for our newsletters.

The Enemy

by Kieran Hurley
after Henrik Ibsen

A National Theatre of Scotland production.
First premiered by National Theatre of Scotland on 13 October 2021 at Dundee
Rep before touring to The King's Theatre Edinburgh, Eden Court Inverness and
Perth Theatre.

Creative Team

Kieran Hurley	Writer
Finn den Hertog	Director
Jen McGinley	Set and Costume Designer
Lewis den Hertog	Video Designer
Katharine Williams	Lighting Designer
Kathryn Joseph	Composer
Matt Padden	Sound Designer
Vicki Manderson	Co-Movement Director
Robbie Gordon	Co-Movement Director
Leonie Rae Gasson	Assistant Director
Laura Donnelly CDG	Casting Director
Rosanna Vize	Original Set Design

Performers

Hannah Donaldson	Kirsten Stockmann
Billy Mack	Derek Kilmartin
Neil McKinven	Benny Hovstad
Taqi Nazeer	Aly Aslaksen
Gabriel Quigley	Vonny Stockmann
Eléna Redmond	Petra Stockmann

Production Team

Alice Black	Production Manager
Amy Dawson	Lighting Supervisor
Jock Dinsdale	Stage Supervisor
Sophie Ferguson	Costume Supervisor
Maddy Grant	Deputy Stage Manager
Ross Hunter	Lighting Programmer
Nicky McKean	Costume Technician
Andy Reid	Video Supervisor
Kat Siebert	Assistant Stage Manager
Andy Stuart	Sound Supervisor
Emma Yeomans	Company Stage Manager

Access

Glenda Carson	Captioner
Amy Cheskin	BSL Performance Interpreter
Emma-Jane McHenry	Audio Describer

National Theatre of Scotland is a Theatre Without Walls.

We don't have our own building. Instead, we bring theatre to you. From the biggest stages to the smallest community halls, we showcase Scottish culture at home and around the world. We have performed in airports and tower blocks, submarines and swimming pools, telling stories in ways you have never seen before.

We want to bring the joy of theatre to everyone. Since we were founded in 2006, we have produced hundreds of shows and toured all over the world. We strive to amplify the voices that need to be heard, tell the stories that need to be told and take work to wherever audiences are to be found.

nationaltheatrescotland.com

Jackie Wylie   Artistic Director and Chief Executive
Seona Reid   DBE Chair

The Enemy

1.

Petra Stockmann *sits at home, duvet wrapped around her, eating a bowl of cereal. Her face is lit in cold blue laptop light.*

Projected video shows an archive montage of old industry, establishment shots of a now-dilapidated small town centre, a post-industrial west of Scotland coastline as corny music plays. Vox pops of present-day citizens of the town:

Citizen 1 To really understand this place, you've got to get to grips with the sheer scale of what was lost. You know? We used to have jobs here. Real jobs. And when that was taken away from us, well – everything else goes with it. Gone.

Citizen 2 The whole identity of the place. Our dignity. The place just gets forgotten about completely. The life expectancy is frightening, criminal really.

Citizen 3 A lot of folk don't stick here. Others maybe don't have a choice, maybe don't think about it much. It's just the way it is here. A shit hole.

Beat.

Citizen 3 I'm allowed to say that cos I'm from here, I hear you saying that and you're in trouble, haha!

Video cuts to **Aly**, *walking the street, talking to the camera.*

Aly As a musician and songwriter, I'm always fascinated by the different meanings of words. We all know that politicians are full of empty buzzwords. 'Innovation.' 'Growth.' 'Regeneration.' But what does it really mean? To regenerate? To bring new life. To be renewed, reformed, and reborn.

Cut to bright images of healthy people swimming, families on flumes, racquet sports, cycling through a forest, etc. Total change of vibe! A massive transformative redevelopment!

Aly It's been a long time coming. And some said it would never happen. But the Big Splash resort will soon be opening its doors to visitors from all across the world! This amazing new holiday resort is a development on an unprecedented scale, combining a water theme park, an expansive health spa complex, an Olympic-standard swimming pool, leisure centre, cultural hub, and a world-leading state-of-the-art indoor beach compound!

Citizen 3   A beach resort! Here! Can you imagine. It's basically a total dream! A ridiculous dream!

Citizen 2   Not just rubbish jobs, like proper employment. Our young folk won't be forced to leave to find work. They're saying we'll actually have people coming *here*, for jobs and quality of life. The reversal is just… it's impossible to even put into words.

Citizen 4   Absolute least this town deserves –

Citizen 5   That's it. That's it.

Citizen 4   One hundred percent.

Citizen 5   We were saying that. It's like winning the World Cup. But God knows we deserve a change in our luck.

Citizen 6   The fact it was the two sisters as well, working to make it happen. A family from here. The story is just – proud. That's what I am. Just so proud of this place.

Citizen 1   Nobody actually thought this would happen! We've been waiting, hoping for years. Years! And it's finally come. It's our time, and we're raring to go! Bring it on! Ha ha! Cheers!

As this plays, action unfolds in various pockets of the stage. **Vonny Stockmann** *emerges, half-dressed. Full-politician garb from the waist up; pyjamas from the waist down.* **Benny Hovstad** – *stony-faced, tired* – *puts on his suit, does his tie in the mirror.* **Derek Kilmartin** *picks up an outsized teddy bear with a bow on it from somewhere and takes a photo of it on his phone.*

Onscreen, **Aly** *and* **Vonny** *stand among a crowd of townsfolk.*

Aly   It's going to cause a real –

Crowd   Big Splash!

Aly *enters the stage space, filming himself on a handheld tripod or selfie stick. He moves effortlessly as he does so, the tech totally natural to him like an extra limb. He is a real pro at this.*

Aly   I'm Aly Aslaksen, and I'll be running a series of bespoke events on all my platforms to coincide with the launch of the Big Splash resort, telling you all you need to know about this transformative development. Why? Because I'm a local boy who cares about the future of the place he came from – that's it. Follow me on Insta, Twitter and TikTok for ongoing updates on the opening of the resort and the bid to have the town named UK City of Regeneration. I'll be doing a set at our digital launch party, sponsored by Kilmartin Industries. So at me with suggestions for my crowd-sourced swimming-themed playlist.

Onstage, **Kirsten Stockmann** *enters, in the same room as* **Petra**.

Aly   Details are appearing on your screen right about now, so smash that like button, watch follow, share, and subscribe –

Kirsten *slaps the laptop shut, the video cuts out. She hurriedly sets about trying to get her stuff together, make* **Petra**'s *lunch, and set up a tablet for a video call.*

Petra   Did you know that teenagers need to get on average around ten hours of sleep a night? And if we don't it can really have all sorts of negative effects.

Kirsten   Uh huh.

Petra   Headaches. Acne. *And* it can seriously impair our neurological functions. Like our ability to absorb information, to problem solve, and like even to just remember basic information like, names, and dates. And homework. So really, from a scientific perspective, forcing us to go into school at this time in the morning is actually not only oppressive but also has an adverse effect on the quality of our education.

Kirsten   It's nearly eight o clock Petra, get dressed.

Petra   It's just science. Just thought you'd be interested maybe in some of the scientific facts about what's going on for your daughter right now. Maybe that's why so many kids are off sick right now. Did you think of that?

Kirsten   Petra, I don't have the time for any of this, okay? Not today, so…

Petra   Ten hours, mum! I don't get anything like that do I? I mean, just think of all the potential I must just be pissing away.

Kirsten   If you want to get more sleep, you can go to bed earlier. Simple.

Petra   Ah, I knew you'd say that. But here's a thing. It is *also* a scientific fact that biological sleep patterns shift towards a later time during adolescence, so it's natural for teenagers to not really be able to get to sleep at all until at least, like, eleven-thirty or whatever. And then that would be like not even waking up until half nine.

Kirsten   Well your mental arithmetic seems to be ticking over just fine for someone with seriously impaired neurological functions.

Petra   That's not even counting, like, if you're awake at night and can't sleep, cos you're thinking about stuff or you're anxious or whatever. Like, to really properly account for that I should definitely be staying in bed until at least noon.

Kirsten   Petra. What's the matter? Are you ill? You don't look ill.

Petra   If I say 'yes' will you let me stay at home, is that how this works?

Kirsten   You didn't drink the tap water did you?

Petra   You said it was probably fine.

Petra*'s phone beeps. She looks at it. The message, projected, reads: 'Hiya weirdo. You gonna be at school today? Will see you later. Bitch.'*

Kirsten   It probably is fine.

Petra   Now that you've got a real job can you at least get me a decent phone? This is embarrassing.

Kirsten   What's the matter?

Petra   Nothing.

Kirsten   Look, I know it's not easy coming in to a new school. You just need to get out there and be yourself okay? It'll get easier.

Just stay true to yourself and the right people will come to you. When I was your age I wanted to go dogging off the whole time too, but –

Petra   What did you call it? Dogging?

Kirsten   Yes.

Petra   Ew.

Kirsten   What kind of mother would I be if I just let you stay off school whenever you felt like it?

Petra   A kind of… great one?

Kirsten *receives a video call.*

Kirsten   Back down here and dressed for school in *five minutes* okay? I've got to take this Skype call. It's your Auntie Vonny.

Petra   Skype? Literally nobody in the world uses Skype.

Kirsten   Your Auntie Vonny does. Now beat it.

The call connects. **Vonny** *appears onscreen. She remains visible in person elsewhere onstage.*

Vonny   Hello? Can you see me alright? Is it working? Now I don't have long –

Kirsten   I can hear you fine. Here we go eh! You excited?

Petra   Hi Auntie Vonny.

Vonny   Oh hiya honey!

Kirsten   Petra. Upstairs. Clothes on. Now.

Petra *sulkily drags herself off.*

Kirsten   She's trying to skive off. Again.

Vonny   How's she settling in, okay?

Kirsten   Ach, you know. Early days. She'll get there. She thinks the other kids single her out, for, you know. Being different.

Vonny   Well Kirsten hen, if you will give her a name like *Petra,*

I mean –

Kirsten   You wanted to talk to me about the speech?

Vonny   Yes.

Kirsten   Can you not use a phone like a normal person?

Vonny   I'm keeping the line free, for a phoner with the BBC.
Then I'm straight over for a livecast with your actual Aly Aslaksen!

Kirsten   Fancy. What's a livecast?

Vonny   I don't know. Have you written it yet?

Kirsten   Nearly.

Vonny   How near is nearly?

Kirsten   How soon is now, Vonny, Christ, I –

Vonny   Could you send me what you have just now? And then
when you do finish, if you could send the finished one over too.
Text me, so I can pick it up straight away –

Kirsten   I wasn't really planning on having anything typed up to
be honest, I thought I'd just go with the flow.

Vonny   No. No, I told you, you need to have it written down so I
can have it all properly checked. I can't have you just shooting from
the hip Kirsten, I know what you're like.

Kirsten   People don't want a big speech, they want to celebrate!
And you know I hate the whole public speaking thing. I'll just say
that it's a privilege to be here, at this historic moment –

Vonny   Good. Good.

Vonny *turns her laptop so the webcam faces the wall, quickly finishes getting
dressed.*

Kirsten   Some nice stuff about you for making this whole thing
a reality –

Vonny   On that.

Vonny *turns the laptop back around and sits down.*

Vonny   I have some suggestions here about what you might try to cover.

Kirsten   You're kidding me on.

Vonny   You can hardly blame me for wanting to keep you on a tight leash, Kirst. This is the most important thing to happen to this town in any of our lifetimes. If you'd sent me your speech weeks ago like I asked you, I wouldn't have to do this.

Kirsten   I've just been a bit distracted alright, I've been busy. Sorry.

Vonny   On what like?

A knock. **Benny Hovstad** *enters, eating a pasty.*

Benny   Kirst! Oop. Sorry. I'm not interrupting am I?

Kirsten   My sister's just beamed herself into my kitchen to dictate my speech to me, it's fine.

Vonny   I am not dictating, I'm –

Benny   Morning Councillor.

Vonny   Provost, if you don't mind Benny.

Benny   Nae bother.

Vonny   I'm not dictating, Kirsten, I'm simply asking you to –

Kirsten   Send it to you to approve or rewrite it and make sure it says nice things about you?

Vonny   It's nothing personal. This is transformative for a lot of people, and they've been waiting a long time for it. We owe it to them, to get this right. We might be frontrunners for City of Regeneration but it's not in the bag yet, so –

Benny   Don't worry Vonny, I'm sure you'll get the political recognition you deserve.

I mean no one's really bothered that it was your sister's idea in the first place –

Vonny   It was not Kirsten's idea! It was a tie! I mean – I mean, we came up with it together. That's what I mean. Benny what in God's name are you eating?

Benny   Steak bake.

Vonny   It's eight o'clock in the morning.

Benny   Correct.

Vonny   You'll be dead before sixty you know that?

Benny   Well. Better fill the remaining mornings with enjoyable breakfasts then.

Vonny   Kirsten you're a founding director of a bloody health centre, tell him.

Kirsten   She's not wrong Benny.

Benny   Priorities but. Did you know that Greggs has a fully unionised workforce? Rarity these days. *And* they have an ever-increasing rate of pay, pegged to inflation. Wee factoid there. Don't get that at your Whole Foods do you? Ethical consumerism in action that's what this is. Up the workers!

Vonny   Not with my digestion. Look, I've got pressers all day, I've got to get on.

Kirsten   Don't let us stop you Vonny.

Vonny   Send me the speech alright?

Vonny *hangs up.*

Benny   Well she's nervous.

Kirsten   Not as nervous as me! Public speaking. Officialdom. Suits and ties and cameras. Gives me the creeps. Petra!

Benny   Do you want to practice on me? I can help.

Kirsten   Thanks, I'll be fine. Face your fears and that. I'll keep it short. Tell them the honest truth. That this is the proudest day of my life. That I never dreamed I'd see these plans become a reality. That it's no less than every one of the people here deserve, and it's a privilege just to be a part of it. Then I'll get out the way so folk can get to the bar!

Benny   You've done this before.

Kirsten *looks at her phone.*

Benny   City of Regeneration eh? Fuck me. They really do stretch the definition of 'city' with these things don't you think? Kirsten?

Kirsten   Hm?

Benny   Candy Crush is it?

Kirsten   What?

Benny   Your phone.

Kirsten   Oh – aye – no. I was just – I was expecting to hear from someone. Sorry. Tea?

Benny   Smashing, aye.

Benny *goes to make the tea.*

Kirsten   No! Sit down. Let me.

Benny *watches, slightly bemused as* **Kirsten** *fills the kettle up from a big bottle of water.*

Benny   Is everything alright Kirsten? You're – you're all – you're all fine here?

Kirsten   Yeah, I mean – it's more than I ever dreamed of, for Petra and me. A proper home, with a garden. Not like that damp shithole we were living in down there. You know I couldn't ever have imagined, when we were wee, that I'd wind up in one of these big houses. Petra's missing her old school and stuff, but she'll get there, you know how kids are.

Benny   Well, if there's anything you need –

Kirsten   I just need to start properly furnishing the place. Decorating. Lampshades. Things like that. That's what folk do, I think.

Benny   I was just checking you're okay – for money and everything –

Kirsten   I'm fine. I'm finally earning something now. We're fine. Really. Thanks though.

Benny   Good good. Life gets easier when you sell out to the man eh?

Kirsten   Hey watch it you. I like to think of it more like growing up, thank you very much. Making actual change, in the real world.

Benny   Absolutely.

Kirsten   I'm not saying we've not had to make some uncomfortable compromises, but that's just –

Benny   I'm yanking your chain, the whole thing is fucking brilliant you know that.

Kirsten   I do.

Benny   You're still giving me my interview later aye?

Kirsten   Course!

Benny   Tremendous. Dr Kirsten Stockmann, the wild child! The prodigal daughter coming home to usher in a bright new dawn!

Kirsten   You can't call me that.

Benny   What?

Kirsten   I'm not a doctor, you know that!

Benny   Ach, nobody cares about stuff like that!

Kirsten   I do. It's the truth.

Benny   It's the story that counts! A big triumphant homecoming, people love that. Come on! Yes!

Benny *grabs* **Kirsten** *and gives her a twirl.* **Kirsten** *laughs.*

Benny   There we go!

Kirsten   You're ridiculous you know that?

Benny   'Scuse me?

Kirsten   You're a ridiculous person.

Benny   I've been called worse. How's Petra?

Kirsten   Is it a stupid name?

Benny   Sorry?

Kirsten   Petra's not a stupid name is it? Is Petra a stupid name?

Benny   Not at all, it's lovely. How?

Kirsten   It's a strong name. It means rock. It's strong.

Petra *enters, wearing her school uniform.*

Petra   It means 'Peter' actually, and yes it is stupid.

Benny   Petra! There she is! How are you darling?

Petra   What's he doing here?

Kirsten   Petra don't be so rude. Here you are Benny.

Benny   Ta, love. Just popping in to say hi, check in on your mum ahead of tonight. You'll be the toast of the school today I should have thought.

Petra   Doubt it. They all hate me. I hate it there.

Kirsten   Petra.

Benny   Ha. Good attitude. I was the same. Hated it. All that keeping your head down, not stepping out of line, regurgitating the same old bollocks. You're a smart girl Petra. Bet you're a right thorn in the side of those teachers. Am I right?

Petra   Mum.

Benny   The important thing is to be an *independent thinker*, that's what they don't teach you. That's the one thing they don't want you to learn, the hypocrites.

Petra *looks at* **Benny**, *openly unimpressed.*

Benny   I only had one teacher I liked. There's always one, I think. Mine was Mr McDonald. History. The rest of the teachers hated him. He was all about teaching young folk to speak truth to power. A romantic old sod maybe, but he meant it. He's the reason I got into journalism, I think. Who's your favourite teacher Petra?

Petra   Dunno. Ms Quinn. Media Studies.

Benny   Media Studies eh? Fantastic. We never got anything like that. Ms Quinn. She's a real inspiration then is she?

Petra   No. She's a supply teacher. She just puts on old films and sits and does the sudoku. I've seen the first forty-five minutes of *Grease*, the first forty-five minutes of *Indiana Jones: Raiders of the Lost Ark*, and the first forty-five minutes of *Labyrinth* with David Bowie. Might watch the second half of that one day actually, I'd quite like to find out what happens to the baby.

Kirsten   Here.

Petra   What's this?

Kirsten   Packed lunch, what's it look like. Benny, let yourself out we have to dash.

Petra   Why are we still doing packed lunches? Bet it's something weird.

Kirsten   I'm not suddenly made of cash Petra. It's not weird, it's a hummus sandwich.

Here, take another one of these.

Petra   A *hummus sandwich*? You do know that's the kind of thing that'll get me my cunt kicked in don't you?

Kirsten   Petra! Jesus!

Petra   What? That's just how they talk here! You're the one that said I had to make an effort to try to fit in!

Kirsten   Just get in the fucking car, will you?

Petra   Nice trousers by the way.

Petra *takes the bottle of water, and exits.*

Kirsten   Is there something wrong with my trousers? What's wrong with my trousers?

Benny   Nothing. They look… magnificent.

Kirsten   These are my best trousers.

Benny   Well it's a day that befits the wearing of one's best trousers.

Kirsten   Exactly.

Benny   I'll see you later aye?

Kirsten   You will. Here.

Kirsten *leaves, tossing house keys to* **Benny**, *who catches them. Alone,* **Benny** *picks up the open water bottle, sniffs its contents, thinks, drinks his tea.*

2.

Kirsten*'s car. It is chucking it outside.*

Petra   He *is* a creep mum, he is such a creep. He is absolutely king of the creeps.

Kirsten   Oh, stop it.

Petra   If he was a famous actor he'd be Meryl Creep.

Kirsten   Benny is an old family friend, and a sweetheart. And he's been a big help getting us settled in, you know that.

Petra   If he was a small French restaurant he would be Un Creeperie.

Kirsten   Petra.

Petra   If he was a Radiohead song he'd be 'Fake Plastic Creeps'.

Kirsten   Enough.

Silence. **Petra** *looks at her phone.*

Kirsten   You'll let me know if there's more off sick today will you?

Petra   Yes.

Kirsten   How many is it now? Eight? Nine?

Petra   Twelve yesterday.

Kirsten   Twelve?

Petra's *phone vibrates.*

Kirsten   Is that me? Is that – Petra will you pass me my phone please?

Petra   It's mine.

The text message on **Petra**'s *phone reads*
Grandad: Gonnae tell your mum I said hi? Joke.

Kirsten   Oh. Right.

Grandad: But serisly. Tell her Im rooting for her and hope launch goes well.

Kirsten   Is that you or –

Petra   Mum, they're all me. Will you chill out.

Kirsten   I'm expecting someone. Who's texting you so much?

Petra   Grandad.

Kirsten   I do wish you wouldn't call him that. He's not your grandad.

Petra   He's my dad's dad isn't he? He says to tell you he hopes it goes well tonight. And that he's rooting for you.

Kirsten   He doesn't mean that. What does he want?

Petra   Nothing.

Kirsten   Derek Kilmartin never wants nothing Petra, what does he want?

Petra   Nothing! We're just chatting.

Petra *texts:*
I told her. She says go fuck yourself, basically.
Grandad: lol course she does
Grandad: Have you been to Gio's yet? Smashing ice cream. Let's meet there.

Petra   He's gonna take me to the ice cream shop at lunchtime.
Aw. Cute.

Grandad: [Ice cream emoji. Sunglasses emoji.]

Petra   Why do you hate him so much?

Kirsten   Can't you just, hang out with your own friends or
something.

Petra   Back in London you mean?

Kirsten   Sorry. I'm just, nervous. Alright? A big day.

The car stops. **Petra** *goes to get out.*

Kirsten   'Creep', by the way. You could have just said 'Creep'.

Petra   What?

Kirsten   Radiohead already have a song called 'Creep'. It would
have worked better if you'd just said 'Creep'.

Petra   Oh. Well I don't know do I, what am I like fifty?

A phone buzzes.

Petra   That one was you.

Petra *leaves.* **Kirsten** *fumbles for her phone. She sees the message. We
see flashes of the subject line on screen, the following words briefly visible:
'URGENT.' 'Tests positive.' 'Contamination.' 'Water.'*

Kirsten   No. No, no, no. No.

3.

Vonny *is filming a livecast interview with* **Aly**, *onstage and projected.
Elsewhere onstage throughout,* **Kirsten** *watches the interview between*
Vonny *and* **Aly**, *visibly anxious. She paces. Reads. Sinks her face into her
hands. Freaks the fuck out.*

Aly   Vonny, you know I gotta say, in the run-up to this a lot
of people were saying to me, 'Aly, it's not really like you to get a
straight-laced politician on the show…'

Vonny   Careful who you're calling 'straight-laced' wee man!

Aly   And that's what I told them! Because you're like me, we both grew up here –

Vonny   Right, yeah.

Aly   And like me, you'll have seen first-hand how the people of this town have been ignored, right? Cast aside by governments –

Vonny   Oh aye, for decades Aly. I was at primary school here in the eighties, and I remember it well – I've seen that legacy of repeated failed promises, and the effect that has had.

Aly   It has to be said, not everyone was delighted about the plans at first. There's been a lot of suspicion, of big developments with big promises, and not without reason either.

Vonny   Of course, and there's always going to be people who want to stoke those sorts of fears, for their own political ends. And so when we looked at the benefits, on health, jobs, tourism – but more than that, on people's *lives* Aly – I just knew it had to happen. And I think people really do see that.

Aly   It's a big deal, it must have been a tough gig getting it over the line.

Vonny   It wasn't always easy, no, but it was a matter of political will. It took imagination and effort. Combing private investment with public funds, pulling it all together by hook or by crook. That's the true spirit of this town, I think. Knowing that sometimes you have to roll up your sleeves and get on with it. And now, tonight's launch event also sees shares floated in the resort for the first time, which we hope will be the start of new investment, new money coming into the town. But we're also inviting you, the citizens of the town, to become shareholders yourselves through our 'Be Big Splash' community buy-in programme – so don't miss out. Aly, delivering the Big Splash Resort is what we promised to do, it's what we were elected to do, and I'm extremely proud to say: it's what we've done.

Aly   That right there is what I'm talking about. Provost, yes.

Thank you.

And you can look forward to hearing much, much more from Vonny Stockmann and her sister Kirsten at the Big Splash resort later tonight as we launch our bid for UK City of Regeneration. Meantime you can find out more about Be Big Splash by following the hashtag #BeBigSplash, and why don't you lovely people get in touch with your own memories of growing up here, or your hopes for our future? Tell us what excites you most about Big Splash. Vonny thanks a million for joining us yeah?

Vonny   Thank you. Uh, party on!

Kirsten *switches the interview off. She takes a deep breath. She decides. She leaves.*

4.

Benny Hovstad's *office. He is sitting idly at his desk, picking unhappily at a salad. He is watching nonsense on the internet. Like a video of a comically bad penalty kick, or someone falling in a lake, or maybe someone doing a tutorial on some ludicrous kitchen hack on TikTok. There is a knock at the door.*

Benny *closes YouTube and opens a live graph of the FTSE 100 as* **Kirsten** *enters.*

Benny   Kirst. You're early.

Beat.

Kirsten   Your receptionist wasn't there, I just thought I'd –

Benny   Is everything okay Kirst, you look like someone's died.

Beat.

Benny   Has someone died?

Kirsten   She's sick is she? Your receptionist?

Benny   What? Aye, aye, dinnae worry about –

Kirsten   She been off long?

Benny   Few days.

Kirsten   Anyone else off sick?

Benny   Um. We've had one or two maybe. Change of weather, like.

Kirsten   There's been twelve kids ill in Petra's class.

Benny   Something going round, I suppose. It happens you know, we never used to make such a big fuss out of it.

Kirsten   Vomiting bile. Nausea. Diarrhoea. A burning in the stomach is what they're saying, like their insides are on fire. Must be over one hundred and fifty off across the whole school.

Benny   What's this about hen? Is Petra okay?

Kirsten   Journalists hear things off the record, right Benny?

Benny   Uh huh?

Kirsten   Like there's a code of practice and everything, so that if I say 'this is off the record' you sort of have to agree. Right?

Benny   Um. Aye, something like that.

Kirsten   And we're friends right?

Benny   For sure.

Beat.

Kirsten   They've been drinking poison. The kids. Your receptionist. Everyone, actually. The water in the town it's, it's, it's toxic. All of it. And we did it. We've poisoned them, Benny. The whole town. Actual poison.

Benny   What?

Beat.

Kirsten   When they were building the resort. They, they re-routed the, the pipes. The town's water infrastructure. The plumbing and stuff. To be able to supply the new development with, with enough, with the, with the –

Benny   Water?

Kirsten   Water. Yes. To get the necessary water supply. For a massive development like this. They were worried that it was holding the thing up okay? But Vonny wanted everything completed on schedule so that we'd be in time to make the bid. For City of, City of, City of –

Benny   City of Regeneration.

Kirsten   City of fucking Regeneration. And I warned them. I tried to warn them and – they rushed it through anyway.

Benny   Rushed what through?

Kirsten   The plumbing. They cut corners, somehow, I don't know. To get it finished on time. And now the water supply is letting in a, a – well it's a toxicity. A contamination.

Benny   Right.

Kirsten   Into the whole town. And that's why your receptionist is off sick. That's why the school is full of empty chairs. And there's only going to be more. I honestly don't know how bad it gets. But I know it's there.

Pause.

Benny   Jesus.

Beat.

Benny   How do you know this?

Kirsten   I had a few samples sent to a lab.

Benny   Samples of what?

Kirsten   Tap water. From my house. And from random spots, across town. One from here actually. And from the Resort. It's contaminated. All of it. And all in the same way.

Benny   And you never thought to mention it before now?

Kirsten   I didn't know anything before now! It was a hunch! I tried to put it out my mind, told myself I was just taking precautions. I expected to hear back weeks ago! I didn't want to set off the alarm without knowing, did I? You know exactly how that story goes. 'Here's Kirsten, stirring up bother again!' You know what my sister's like, she'd never have listened!

Benny   But you cannae like – the water looks fine. It tastes fine. Smells fine. You cannae see it or that.

Kirsten   No Benny you can't bloody see it!

Benny   Well where's it coming from? The – the fucking – contamination. The poison.

Kirsten   I can't prove that yet but it seems obvious doesn't it? Think of the nearest literal cesspit.

Pause.

Benny   Derek Kilmartin's land. The dump.

Kirsten *nods.*

Benny   Oh ya fucker. Well. This is awkward for yous.

Kirsten   Petra is seeing him today. She insists on calling him 'grandad.'

Benny   Eesh. And you're sure – like absolutely sure – that the water's –

Kirsten   One hundred percent.

Benny   When did you get the tests back?

Kirsten   Today. Got the email this morning. After I saw you.

Benny   And what did it say?

Kirsten   That it's fucked. The water's fucked. We're fucked.

Silence.

Benny   Wow.

Pause.

Benny What do we about the resort? I mean people are, people are expecting that – I mean it can't. It can't now. It's gonna have to – they can't open now can they? They'll have to shut it down?

Beat.

Benny Oh shite.

Kirsten I don't know how we're going to tell them.

Silence. **Kirsten** *stares at* **Benny**, *desperate.*

Benny Here. Look. Right. Okay. Right. Look. At least we know now right? I mean really, to know and do something about it, than not know at all. You've done brilliantly here Kirst, actually. This, look, this is good. This is good. Think about it. If you hadn't found this out this could have been even worse, like, really really bad –

Kirsten Yes. Aye. Disastrous.

Benny Well, you've just saved the day Kirsten! Thank God you're here, or we'd all be even more screwed. You've said lives, probably –

Kirsten I need to tell Vonny, it'll crush her –

Benny Crush her! She's gonna kiss you! You've just rescued her political career! Imagine she'd gone and cracked on with the whole thing, not knowing this. She'd be toast. Fuck, she'll probably try to make out the whole thing was her discovery!

Kirsten You don't think people will be furious? They will, they'll be fucking furious!

Benny Aye maybe, but they're always furious! And anyway, only if it's put to them the wrong way. Was it Vonny's fault that Kilmartin's been letting his corporate mates dump their shite around the town while everyone turns a blind eye? No. It's the fault of the, I dunno, government, probably. Or even better, the previous council. Isn't it?

Kirsten Yeah, but that's not really –

Benny Something has to be done! Right? As soon everyone understands that this is a crisis averted, they'll be over the moon with relief! Wouldn't you?

Kirsten   And if it, if it all falls through, the resort, my job and everything I mean, then…

Benny   It won't! They'll figure all that out. Temporary repairs. You're gonna be a local hero doll. 'There goes the lassie that saved us all from drinking Kilmartin's toxic death juice!' You'll never have to buy a drink in this town again Kirsten, this is huge.

Kirsten   Right, well, I mean –

Benny   Yes! Come on! This is great. We'll help. We'll run a big piece on it for you, get the word out –

Kirsten   I was speaking off the record Benny.

Benny   Of course! And I would never – you know that. But we're gonna have to act fast. And people are gonna have to know aren't they?

Kirsten   Yes, they are.

Benny   Well then. You just say the word. The sooner the better, so we can seize control of the story. Proper investigative journalism for a change, a big scoop. Real light in the darkness stuff, like the old days man. Yes! It should be in your words though. Can you get something to me by this afternoon?

Kirsten   Well – yes, right aye. Thank you Benny. Thank you. I'll be in touch. Thank you!

Benny   You're a hero, Kirsten. A hero!

5.

A cafe. **Petra** *sits with* **Derek***, next to the teddy bear and a Knickerbocker Glory the size of a small house.*

Derek   The truth is Petra, I've always liked your mother. I have. She was always a trouble maker even when she was much younger, you know that? Getting involved in her protests and all that business. Did she ever tell you about the time she organised a school walk-out against the Iraq war?

Petra *shakes her head.*

Derek She must've been about your age. The teachers got wind of it a few days before, threatened everyone with a month's worth of lunchtime detentions. So when your mum heard that everyone else had bottled it and nobody was gonna join her, she just went into school early that day. Chained herself to the gates with a bike lock so no one could get in. School was shut the whole day, they had to get in the fire brigade to cut her loose!

Petra *chuckles.*

Derek Aye, she didn't take nonsense from anyone. Can't say I always agreed with her *beliefs* and everything but she had spunk. I admired that. I think that's what my Andy liked about her too.

Petra I wish I could have met him.

Derek I wish you could have too. Sometimes. But then I remember what an awful prick he was and I think well, maybe it's best you never. Course I tried to help your mum after she took you down south. Offered her money and stuff. She tell you that? Thought not. She wouldn't take it. Said it was dirty money, coming from a dirty great big businessman like me. She had all her environmental *principles* and things. Then she had all the legal fees from the protests and that, still wouldnae take it so she had to work twice as hard –

Petra She's a fucking idiot!

Derek Well, I'm glad you're back. I know you're too old for teddy bears and stuff, I just – want to make up for all the lost years of buying you nice things. You're here now. Time to make things right. Here, your tea's getting cold.

Petra Oh – I can't have it, sorry.

Derek Why's that?

Petra Mum won't let me. Made me promise.

Derek   It's fairtrade, probably. They're all fairtrade these days.

Petra   No it's – she's made me promise not to drink the tap water.

Derek   Eh? The water here is magic. Much better than the waxy, chalky, lukewarm London piss you're used to. Tastes lovely and crisp and freezing right out the tap.

Petra   She says it's making everyone sick.

Derek   Really?

Petra   I think it's part of her ongoing mission to make sure everyone at school singles me out as a little weirdo. Sometimes think if my dad was here I'd fit in more.

Derek   It's just your accent love, that's all.

Petra   Cheers Grandad.

Derek   They'll get over it once they get to know you. It's just they think it puts you up here you know? With them down there. And they hate that.

Petra   I'm not posh.

Derek   That's just not how they see it though. And if there's one thing folk in this town can't stand it's when they think someone's acting like they're above them. Because people here hate success. It's a sickness they have, a kind of jealousy. Unless you're doing an Aly Arselicker, some pop star or whatever he is doing some charity drive, on the internet, prancing like a tit. They love that. Here, eat your ice cream. You've not touched it.

Petra   It's the campest thing I've ever seen in my life, look at it. I'm scared to touch it, in case it breaks into song.

Derek   That's a proper Knickerbocker Glory love, that's what that is. Homemade Scottish Italian ice cream made by the same family for four generations. You don't get that in your bloody Shoreditch, do you?

Petra   Mm. It's really good.

Derek   Told you.

Petra   Have some.

Derek   No, it's yours, it's for you, it's a present.

Petra   I can't eat all of this I'll be sick, here.

Derek   Oh go on then. Oh, fucking hell. 'Scuse me.

They both laugh as **Derek** *tries to eat a bigger scoop of ice cream than his tiny spoon can manage.*

Derek   Bloody hell that's good. Here.

Derek *helps himself to some more.* **Petra** *laughs.*

Derek   So here, tell me about this tap water thing?

6.

Kirsten *sits at home, typing at her laptop. She is on the phone, to* **Benny** *who sits elsewhere onstage with* **Aly**.

Kirsten   Aye, I'm nearly finished. I couldn't get through to Vonny. Sent her an email. She text to say she's coming round, she's on her way over now.

Benny   Just a text? Weird. She'll be buying time to think about how she can take the credit for saving the day no doubt.

Kirsten   Probably. I don't mind to be honest. I think it's pretty good what I've got here, it might be a bit over-long and a bit heavy on the sort of science speech –

Benny   Don't worry about that. I can help with all of that. Just get me the bloody thing. Here, there's someone I want you to meet.

Kirsten   Who? Who?

Benny   Only one Aly Aslaksen, he's raring to say hi –

Kirsten   Benny fucking hell, we said off the record, no one else is supposed to know yet, Vonny's not even –

Benny   It's cool, it's cool, it is off the record. I'm just, you know, getting our ducks in a row for when we make the big splash – uh, no pun intended – here – someone wants to say hello –

Aly   Hiya there Kirsten.

Kirsten   Oh, hi –

Aly   Benny's given me the whole scoop. It's really fucking bad right?

Kirsten   I'm afraid so. I'm so sorry.

Aly   No, no. It's – it's good you've found this out. Because now we can start to turn this oil tanker around right?

Kirsten   Yes, exactly, it's quite urgent.

Aly   Well, as I've said to Benny already, I'm very happy to help. I know I'm just some podcast guy, I'm not a scientist or anything like you, but I do have a bit of a following in these parts. You know, I saw this documentary about Flint, Michigan? If we wanted to do some high profile awareness raising shit –

Kirsten   I don't think any of that will be necessary yet.

Aly   Oh of course, I'm just spit-balling ideas you know –

Kirsten   What about the launch tonight?

Aly   Yeah. Talk to your sister. Let's find out. If we cancel we cancel, obviously. I mean no one's gonna pretend it's not a ball-ache, but needs must. I think that once everyone's up to speed then maybe it's okay. We could use the launch as a ready-made platform, to let people know. People of the town all there, people tuned in online, gathered press –

Kirsten   Okay. Okay. Great.

Aly   You're gonna need to re-write your speech though! You're the main event now Kirsten. The hero, Benny tells me. 'We could be heroes, just for one day!' Ha. Except, longer, because you're gonna make a really lasting impact on people's general wellbeing and so forth. Listen I have to dash, I've got my Twitch stream coming up –

Kirsten   Not a word of this okay, please don't mention –

Aly   Lips. Sealed. Awaiting further instructions Commander. If there's anything I can do to help, I've got your number from Benny here I'm gonna text you mine alright. Be in touch. We're all behind you in this. The whole town *will* be behind you on this. I promise.

Kirsten   Thank you. Thank you, Aly. I really appreciate your help. It means a lot.

Aly   Ha ha, no problemo Kirsten. Ciao.

Benny   See you Aly.

Aly   Ta ta Benzo.

Aly *leaves.*

Benny   You still there?

Kirsten   You weren't meant to tell anyone. Benzo.

Benny   Och, come on. Aly's not gonna go rogue with this. He's a fanny. All hot air and wish trees, following around his trendy causes like he's fucking Bono. But, people here genuinely listen to him.

Kirsten   It was nice of him to say 'the whole town is behind you.' That was very sweet.

Benny   Alright Mrs 'I had your poster on my wall' keep your knickers on. The whole town will be behind you! You can count on us. Okay?

A knock at the door.

Kirsten   That's her.

It's not locked Vonny, come in.

Derek *enters. Face mask around his chin, perhaps.*

Kirsten   Benny I've got to go.

Kirsten *hangs up. She looks up. She sees* **Derek**.

Kirsten   What do you want?

Derek   No need to be rude. I won't stay long, don't worry. Is it true?

Kirsten   Is what true?

Derek   This moonshine of yours about wee beasties living in the taps.

Kirsten   Sorry? Who have you been speaking to?

Derek   Petra. She says you won't let her drink the tap water. Don't be angry at her, she was just trying to look after her grandfather.

Kirsten   I don't know what you're talking about.

Derek   The tap water here is magic. You know that. She says you're worried it's making people sick.

Kirsten   You know something, I would appreciate if you would give her a bit of space. I don't like how you're crowding her out, she's –

Derek   I'm just trying to make her feel welcome.

Kirsten   You can't just buy your way into this family all of a sudden, I made that very, very clear –

Derek   Of course.

Beat.

Derek   So, wee beasties in the water is it? Brilliant.

Kirsten   I don't know what you're talking about –

Derek   What, like cockroaches or something aye? Living in the plumbing! I know me and you have never seen eye to eye, but these wee beasties of yours wouldn't have anything to do with the fact I've got quite a lot invested in this resort would they?

Kirsten   Not beasties. Toxins. And no, that's a ludicrous thing to say.

Derek   Toxins. Right. And it's just you that can see them is it? Using, what, science? And magic woo-woo?

Kirsten   No. Nobody can see it. It's a microscopic contamination, it's – nobody can see it, that doesn't mean it's not there –

Derek   Nobody can see it but that doesn't mean it's not there!
Like God. Or a fart! And you know where they're coming from do
you? You know how they got in there, these magic beasties?

Beat.

Kirsten   Not yet.

Beat.

Derek   Okay then.

Beat.

Derek   Listen, I don't know why you're doing this but if you
think it will embarrass your sister, or send me up and hurt me in
some way then it's a bit of a kamikaze way of going about it –

Kirsten   None of this is fun for me Derek, but it's real. And I will
prove to you that it's real –

Vonny *enters.*

Derek   Well don't let me stand in your way. Oh. Hiya Vonny.

Vonny   Mr Kilmartin,

Derek   Right. I was on my way anyway. Cheerio lassies.

Wee beasties! Ha!

Derek *leaves.*

Vonny   What's he talking about?

Kirsten   Nothing. Petra's been seeing a lot of him. I was asking
him to back off. That's all.

Vonny   Right.

Beat.

Vonny   I got your email.

Kirsten   You've read it I take it?

Vonny   Oh aye. Aye.

Kirsten   Don't worry I'm not gonna do a whole 'I told you so' thing, let's just start where we are and work on fixing this. I think we have to count ourselves lucky that we found out when we did, before it gets much worse –

Vonny   I mean it's not *wonderful* timing. It's not like we had anything planned for later on this evening or that.

Kirsten   I only got the test results today. I know, that is a bit of a nightmare obviously.

Vonny   Was it really necessary? For you to go making these wee investigations behind my back?

Kirsten   It was just speculative. Precautionary. I didn't want to say anything until I was certain, I knew how much you wanted me not to rock the boat and *disrupt things*.

Vonny   And you're certain now then?

Kirsten   Oh, absolutely.

Vonny   Right. And, I'm imagining you're going to want to take this to the board, and to the council. In some kind of official form?

Kirsten   Yes, of course.

Vonny   In your email you use some, pretty colourful language. 'An uninterrupted and unending stream of poison into the whole town.' It's, well it's –

Kirsten   It's what it is. Whether you drink it, swim in it, sit in a bloody steam room with it, that's what it is.

Vonny   And your solution would be, what? To shut down the whole water supply? And re-route the plumbing serving the entire town?

Kirsten   Unless you've a better idea? And we'll need to issue some kind of cease and desist notice to Kilmartin too, and quickly. Stop him letting out his land for dumping industrial waste. It's criminal –

Vonny   'We'll' need to issue a cease and desist?

Kirsten You. You will.

Vonny I don't like Kilmartin any more than you do but that's a licensed waste disposal plant he runs –

Kirsten You're having me on Vonny.

Vonny I don't have the authority to just go around shutting down businesses with impunity Kirsten, I'm a local councillor I'm not bloody Mugabe. Now this, this, plumbing work you propose. The water providers will have their own view on that I imagine, but you're aware that even the workaround is likely to cost a few quid, yes?

Kirsten I'm not a wee kid Vonny, of course 'I'm aware' of that.

Vonny Like, a few million quid.

Kirsten Well, we have to find the money from somewhere then.

Vonny 'We' again, is it?

Kirsten You. You do.

Vonny Right.

Kirsten I can help. I'm sure people will want to help.

Vonny Great. Like how?

Kirsten Crowdfunding. I dunno, I've not really –

Vonny The compensation to local business, the bureaucracy processing all of that – that costs money. Daily deliveries of bottled water to every home, every business. Running that operation, that's a cost. A massive one. Is that coming from the same GoFundMe page or is that separate?

Kirsten It'd only be temporary. And it just has to be done. Political will and all that.

Vonny We don't have any money, Kirsten.

Kirsten Then, the government will have to step in.

Vonny Sure, aye. I'll just ring them up. Off the back of what, some tests run in your mate's lab on the fly? That'll do it.

Kirsten You can commission a fuller investigation, obviously if that's what you need but you need to turn the taps off first because we already know that it's poison –

Vonny Turn the taps off. Cute. And do you know how long it'll take? To 'turn the taps off' and install an alternative water infrastructure, in this manner you suggest?

Kirsten No. A long time. Obviously.

Vonny About two years I should have thought, all in. Maybe three. That's if it all goes without a snag. And what do we do with the Resort in that time, eh?

Kirsten Well we'd have to shut it, obviously.

Vonny Obviously.

Kirsten It would only be temporary –

Vonny And do you suppose anybody would want to come to the place after we re-opened? What sort of advertising campaign do you imagine I might run in order to entice tourists to this, our supposedly life-giving health spa, once the town's reputation as an unbearable toxic shit hole has been fully established in the national press?

Kirsten But that's what it is Vonny, those are just the facts –

Vonny And at this juncture too? On the day we're about to launch an extremely expensive bid in a nationwide competition to recognise us as the best regeneration project in the fucking country? When I've been busting a gut in the press to get the message out that this town is open for business, and when people have been sitting up and taking notice of the fact that we even *exist* for the first time since the seventies! Honestly Kirsten. I knew that bringing you up here was a risk. That you might use your position to do something stupid and destructive. But I didn't quite imagine it would be on such a fucking existential scale. This is something, this really is quite something even for you.

Kirsten This isn't about me, it's about the whole town.

Vonny   It is precisely and only because of the resort that this
town has any future worth talking about, and you know that.

Kirsten   People are getting extremely sick right now Vonny, as
we speak. There are kids, children who are –

Vonny   I'm not convinced the matter is as serious as you've made
it out to be.

Kirsten   As serious! If anything it's worse! They're only ill for
now, but when they start dying Vonny, what then?

Vonny   I don't think you have sufficient proof for such a massive
undertaking.

Kirsten   I have proof that the water is toxic. And people. Are.
Already. Sick.

Vonny   Do you even have any idea of the absolute litany of
health problems that plague a community like ours, all the time?
Do you have any idea what decades of neglect does to the health
of a place like this? The people round here have been shat on,
forever, and I for one remain committed to turning that around.
Some of us actually stuck around here, and we don't need your
outlandish theories. These people aren't sick because they're
poisoned Kirsten. They're sick because they're poor.

Kirsten   You're being astonishingly irresponsible.

Vonny   No. No. I'm doing the only responsible thing. In light
of all factors. All variables. We open the resort as planned. There
is too much at stake, and not enough evidence to justify changing
course at this stage. We tell nobody about this – for now. I will of
course, as you say, commission some further investigations into
what you think you've discovered here. I will raise it with the board
of the resort, privately, when the time is right. But until then not a
word of this gets out to anyone else –

Kirsten   Bit late for that I'm afraid, sorry.

Vonny   Who? Kirsten, who? No. Not Benny fucking Hovstad
Kirsten, come on.

Kirsten   Fraid so. And boy is he keen. All that chest-thumping, greater purpose stuff. It's got him fired right up so it has.

Vonny   You went straight to the fucking press, before you even told *me* –

Kirsten   I spoke to him as friend. It is off the record –

Vonny   Christ you've really absolutely no idea how any of this works do you?

Beat.

Vonny   And you never even think of the damage all this could do to yourself? Eh?

Kirsten   At least I understand there are more important things than my own reputation –

Vonny   Well la-di-fucking-da. I think you're in danger of forgetting what side your bread is buttered on here. Was it not me that sent money to help you when you were putting yourself through university *pursuing your dreams*? Do you think I would have been able to afford to do *any* of that without having spent my life maintaining the integrity of my professional reputation?

Kirsten   I'm grateful for all that but this is bigger than –

Vonny   And now you want to talk to me about 'looking after my reputation' as if that is somehow a dirty, shitey thing to do? Grow up! Who do you think made sure you got this bloody job in the first place?

Kirsten   I got the job on merit, the resort was my idea, it was outlined in my PhD thesis –

Vonny   Failed PhD thesis. You know what I think, I think you got bored. I think things were looking too settled for you so you had to kick shite around the place to create a bit of drama –

Kirsten   Oh fuck off. You can't just sit on something like this, you're going to have to deal with it sooner or –

Vonny   I want you to prepare a full retraction, to be published in the event that questions start to be asked.

Kirsten   What?

Vonny   Now you've let the word out, we've got to be prepared. You'll say the situation is not as critical as you once feared, and that there is no cause for alarm.

Kirsten   Vonny, listen. I deal in public health okay, I can't just – I have a right, in a free society to speak my mind. And people have a basic right to know the truth –

Vonny   Wind your fucking neck in Kirsten! This is my job. Putting out fires like this is what I do, and I'm good at it. And I really don't want this to have to get ugly sis, I really, really don't.

Kirsten   You've made up your mind about this then?

Vonny   I don't believe there is sufficient evidence for such a drastic course of action.

Kirsten   Okay. Fine.

Vonny   We'll look into this, privately, and within a reasonable budget.

Kirsten   Right.

Vonny   And in the meantime, we're pressing on with things as they are. Send me your speech as soon it's done, okay?

Kirsten   Okay.

Vonny   Okay. Good. It's good you're so principled, Kirsten. There's just proper ways of going about things that's all. Just leave that stuff to me, alright? You'll get there.

Kirsten   Got it.

Vonny   Okay. No hard feelings. A big day ahead, we all need to be on the same team.

Kirsten   What's next for you today then?

Vonny   Committee meeting. Then more interviews. Then over to the resort for a site visit before tonight –

Kirsten   Busy.

Vonny   Aye.

Kirsten   Let me fix you a cup of tea –

Vonny   No, no thanks, I have to be off –

Kirsten   A cold drink then – won't take a second. Here.

Kirsten *pours a full pint of water from the tap. She sets it down in front of* **Vonny**.

Kirsten   You have to stay hydrated, Vonny. Can't have you getting a headache.

Beat.

Kirsten   Come on, drink it.

Vonny   Kirsten.

Kirsten   What? If it's fine it's fine, isn't it? Thirsty, tiring work this, serving the people. So better drink up.

Vonny   I don't have to play this childish wee game.

Kirsten   Drink it.

Pause.

Vonny   I'm not thirsty.

Kirsten   Right. I'll add that to my statement will I? 'The situation is not as critical as I once feared and there is no cause for alarm. If you see the Provost Vonny Stockmann refusing tap water, it's simply because she's not thirsty.'

Vonny   You're being ridiculous.

Kirsten   Drink it then. Drink it and I'll write your statement.

Pause. **Vonny** *picks up the glass.*

Vonny   Fine then.

She chucks its contents back into the sink.

Vonny   We'll do it your way.

Kirsten   Okey dokey.

Vonny   You don't get to push me around Kirsten. I tried to warn you. Good luck.

Vonny *leaves.*

Kirsten *takes out her phone. She opens WhatsApp, and messages* **Benny***.*
The text reads:
Kirsten: I spoke to my sister. Not good.
Grey tick. Two grey ticks. A wait. The ticks all turn blue.
Benny: Ah.
Kirsten: Pretty spectacularly not good.
Benny: Right.
Kirsten: So I guess it looks like we've got a fight on our hands then, eh?
Benny: Yas! Fucking come on then! [Flame emoji.]
Kirsten: Too right. Fuck her. [Fist bump emoji.]

7.

A barrage of social media posts, vox-pops, radio call-ins, responses to **Aly***'s #BigSplashLaunch hashtag. A digital whirlwind of anticipation and excitement. 'Best thing to happen in this Town in generations, no question.' 'New jobs, a brighter future, and hopefully our new visitors can get a different, more positive view of the place.' 'Aly, if I could just say, I started my new job on the resort a few weeks ago and so I've seen all behind the scenes and that, and can I just say it is just absolutely fantastic…'*

Aly   Yes folks, great stuff all this. Just a rumour that we might have some major news coming in that is relevant to today's revelries. Can't say any more for now, but some pretty big, big news. Stay tuned so that you're not the last to know –

Vonny*'s car.* **Vonny** *sits in the passenger seat, alone.* **Benny** *arrives, outside. He looks over his shoulder, and enters.* **Vonny** *hands him hand sanitiser. He obliges.*

Benny　This is all a bit fucking clandestine is it no? You got me something juicy? Can I say a 'senior source'?

Vonny　I spoke to my sister.

Benny　Right. Aye? How's she getting on, how's the speech coming on?

Vonny　Don't be an arsehole, Benny.

Benny　What?

Vonny　I know about the story.

Benny　What story?

Vonny　I don't want this to get difficult Benny, you know that. I really don't. I want you to help me do the right thing here. My sister has the situation completely blown out of proportion –

Benny　Here, listen here I'm a journalist and last I checked we don't talk to politicians about what stories we are or aren't going to run in advance in this country –

Vonny　It's death to this town, Benny. I know you don't want that. Without the resort it –

Benny　Ach, don't give me that, the town'll be fine. Well it'll be shite, but just the same level of shite. You're scared about what this means for you. Well, fair enough. I still think you could make good on this, if you get out on the front foot –

Vonny　I'm not giving you a fucking interview if that's what you mean.

Benny　Suit yourself.

Vonny　You have to kill the story Benny.

Benny　Because what, you say so?

Vonny　Well I was hoping to appeal to your basic sense of right and wrong first, but okay then. Fine. Because I say so.

Benny　Like she cannae just go ahead and post whatever she wants online anyway, I'm just trying to get in on it –

Vonny   Aye but there are *ways* of putting ideas in their proper *context* and that is something that you can help me with –

Benny   Don't patronise me Vonny, love. I don't know what you think this is with your shady wee meetings in poxy wee car parks like you're in the fucking *Wire*, but see if you think for a minute that Benny Hovstad is such a shitey journalist that he'd suppress information in the clear public interest to further the career of some wee smout of a politician, then you'd better think again, alright? Your wee sister has done an important, brilliant thing here. And she deserves our support.

Vonny   Are you finished?

Benny   No, actually, I'm not finished. We've got a free press in case you forgot. The most vital function of democracy. This stuff is what people like me live for, this is the stuff that's in our blood. Speaking truth to power. And you, sweetheart, are about to get your first big taste of what it feels like to be in power and have the truth spoken to you. Right in your stupid wee face. So there. Aye. Now I'm done. If this is all you've got here then I am done with you. So take your wee power flex and shove it up your arse. Ya stuck up cow.

Vonny   You think I don't know about the intern lassies, Benny?

Beat.

Vonny   I mean, if you're done you're done of course but I just thought you might be interested in these emails I happen to have here. Oh. You're staying. Okay good. Well. This one here is from a lassie telling me about how you used to grab her arse every morning. She also has a heartwarming story about being sent to the shops to buy you some johnnies before the staff night out –

Benny   Come on. Show me that. When are these from, these are what, fifteen-year-old these stories I bet you. Workplace banter. Old school maybe, not proud of it but that's the way it was. If this is your idea some kind of kompromat then –

Vonny   This one talks about 'an archaic and dehumanising culture of male entitlement,' that was from someone who worked with you in 2019. She says it was 'a belittling and degrading environment for unpaid female employees.'

Benny   Unpaid! We're broke! Why do you think we relocated back to this shit-hole. Do you have any idea how many journalists we've laid off in the last five years, we cannae pay bloody interns for God's sake!

Vonny   Spoken like a true union man, well done. Solidarity forever. It says here she was scared to say anything because you would ruin her career, but left the job with such a damaged sense of self-worth that she never worked again anyway. Look at this. 'He used to come in to work smelling of booze, it was frightening to be around him. On one occasion, with nobody around, he told me to cheer up and give him a kiss, and when I refused he forced his tongue into my throat – '

Benny   Never happened. Dunno who the fuck she is or what she's talking about, lying wee bitch.

Vonny   Steady on big man. These lying wee bitches have also passed me this.

She shows **Benny** *a picture on her phone.*

Benny   I WAS DRUNK. IT WAS SENT IN ERROR, IT WASN'T EVEN ME WHO –

Vonny   That was sent from your email account, to every single member of staff including –

Benny   I was very, very drunk – it was the Christmas party, there was a few of us just arsing about, I made a full apology, we dealt with –

Vonny   – including an intern who had not yet turned seventeen. A schoolgirl, working weekends. Not legally a child. But about as close as it comes.

Silence.

Benny   I don't appreciate being threatened like this, this is not –

Vonny   I don't see it as a threat Benny. More like a peace offering.

See, it'd be nice if we could stay pals wouldn't it? It's good to have friends isn't it? People to look out for you. See your old mucker here has managed to convince these women to stay quiet for now –

Benny   How?

Vonny   Ways and means.

Benny   Ways and means?

Vonny   Ways and fucking means Benny, aye.

Benny   What ways and means like?

Vonny   I don't need to tell you that, that's my business. You're welcome by the way. Suffice to say it involves a cast-iron guarantee that no women working under you will have to suffer anything like this ever again, which seems fair. But there are also some conditions for me –

Benny   You're bluffing. If anyone is gonna make a noise over any of this nonsense they'd have done it by now, or they'll do it anyway, you don't have any sway over this at all. Nice try.

Vonny   Okay. Okay, fine so let's find out. You go public with your story, and tomorrow I'll go public with mine. Since I don't have any control over the situation anyway, what difference does it make, right? Or, we could go with my suggestion. And see if all of this stays under wraps.

Beat.

Vonny   Ways and means, Benny. Let's stay pals. Okay? Don't run the fucking story.

8.

Kirsten *and* **Benny**, *in a quiet corner of a pub.*

Kirsten   – I think you are going to absolutely love me by the way, because this is really actually quite good. Fuck it, it's *really* good. Listen to this bit: 'That this corruption of our water, our most fundamental life source, looks to have been caused by the council fast-tracking a project that was intended to promote health and wellbeing adds cruel insult to an already deep and violent injury.' Boom! Do you think my sister would have let me write that? No chance. You know what, I'm glad – I am actually glad that she decided to be a dick about it. Imagine we'd had to dance around her the whole time? This way we just get to tell the truth. The simple, uncompromising, honest *truth*. Isn't that the absolute least people deserve? 'The light of truth has been cast over some of the darker corners of this town and it's a light that will now surely only grow. Who knows where it will lead us?' Ha! Take that Vonny, ya cow.

Benny   Kirsten.

Kirsten   I know, I know. I know that you and Aly are both wanting to put me front and centre in this, make me into some kind of hero of the story and all that –

Benny   Kirst –

Kirsten   – I mean I'm not saying I'm not a hero, maybe I am a hero. I mean why not?

Benny   We're not –

Kirsten   You'd accept being the hero, if it was your discovery, wouldn't you? Too right. Aly would. Why should I pretend I'm not a hero? Well fine. Fine then. If people want to call me a hero why shouldn't they?

Benny   We're not running it Kirsten. The story. We're not running it.

Kirsten   What do you mean?

Benny   I can't explain just now. I will later, I promise. I'm really sorry for leading you on. But it's a bad idea. The story is a very bad idea. That's all you need to know. I'm sorry.

Kirsten   No, no, no, no – no. No. No. It's a *good* idea. A *good* idea Benny remember? Speaking truth to power!

Benny   I'll explain later. I've brought Aly up to speed. I got ahead of myself, and I apologise.

Kirsten   What's happened?

Benny   On reflection, I suppose, I don't think you have sufficient proof for such a massive undertaking.

Benny*'s phone beeps. He looks. Projected text: 'Vonny: let me know how you go. If she goes ahead anyway, I have a plan.' His face sinks.*

Kirsten   What's she done? Come on tell me, what has she said to you?

Benny   Who?

Kirsten   Unbelievable. Right. Right, fine. I'll do it without you then. No bother Benny. No bother at all.

Benny   Kirsten. I'm speaking as your friend here, and you need to listen to me. Have you thought about your own position, in all of this?

Kirsten   The truth is the thing that matters and we need to get it out fast, that's what *you* said –

Benny   You are in over your head. Okay? That's the clearest warning I can give you. If you keep pursuing this –

Kirsten   There is *literal fucking poison* coming out of your kitchen taps Benny are you mental?

Benny   What I'm saying is that on reflection I don't think you have sufficient proof for such a –

Kirsten   Oh Jesus Christ!

Benny   We're dropping the story Kirsten, and so should you.

Kirsten *gathers up her stuff.*

Benny   Don't do anything stupid. Kirsten.

Kirsten *leaves.*

9.

Kirsten, *staring at her laptop screen, which we see projected; an unpublished Medium post entitled 'What Lies Beneath: The Truth About The Big Splash Resort And The Poison In YOUR Water by Kirsten Stockmann'. The cursor hovers over the 'publish' button. She stares, deliberating.*

Vonny *stands behind a camera in front of* **Aly**, *who is hurriedly adjusting himself. She gives him a thumbs up.*

Aly   Hey troops, just logging back on with a brief announcement from the people at the Big Splash resort who've asked us to read this short statement to keep you all in the loop with some developments. Here goes.

'We at Big Splash Holiday Resort are sad and sorry to announce that one of our founding Executive Directors, Kirsten Stockmann, has stepped down from upcoming duties on the grounds of emotional and mental health difficulties. We wish Kirsten all the best in dealing with these personal issues, and ask that you respect her privacy.

The launch of the resort will go ahead as planned tonight in conjunction with the launch of the town's bid for UK City of Regeneration, though Ms Stockmann will of course no longer be in attendance. We're all sure Kirsten would want it to go *swimmingly* and for it to be as wonderful a celebration of this town as possible.'

Well. Not the news I expected to be bringing you there and uh, very sad news. I'm honoured to know Kirsten personally myself having met her recently and I extend my warmest wishes to her, and her family.

Petra *looks at her phone. She is horror-struck.* **Vonny** *switches the camera off.*

Aly   So here what the fu –

Vonny   It's fine. It's all fine, don't worry. You look great.

Kirsten   Fuck em.

Kirsten *hits send. Her piece is published. It's out there. She takes a deep breath.*

Benny *looks at his phone.*

Benny   Ah, bollocks.

Benny *calls* **Vonny**. **Vonny** *picks up.*

Benny   She's done it. She's published the story.

Vonny   Course she has.

Benny   She's tagged in all the national news outlets, the council, government, everyone.

Vonny   So take control of the situation then.

Vonny *hangs up.*

Benny   Ah Christ!

10.

An overlapping multimedia cacophony of voices. Audio snatches from radio phone-ins: 'I mean she's mental. I know you cannae say that anymore but that's what they've said. If she's saying this mad stuff then that's a shame for her like, but that's all it is –' 'Look, the thing is, if there's any doubt about it all we need to get it checked out don't we? What are the council doing? Are we getting bottled water delivered? Are we nothing!' 'I went to school with her and there was always something wrong with her, she had this, this evil energy about her…' 'She practically got given the job by her sister it's gross nepotism…' etc. Fragments of news footage; **Aly** *singing to adoring fans at an open mic night as a regional news reporter narrates recent developments. Shaky camera-phone footage posted online; some schoolkids harassing* **Petra** *for her mum being mental, chucking water at her, she throws out a hand and wipes the screen. Concerned messages in a school parents WhatsApp group: 'He's not been able to eat for days. They don't know what's wrong. He's screaming saying he feels like he's burning inside.' 'They've taken her into hospital, she's being fed on a drip. They said she's lucky to be there, they're running out of beds…' Scrolling projections of social media posts and below-the-line article comments: 'Here what if she has a point? Will you be having a shower tonight? I won't! This needs investigated!' 'I don't see anything wrong with the water. Tired of being patronised by so-called experts.' 'Why can't we just have nice things in this* *town without some London wanker turning it into a story about us all drinking piss or whatever. I hate this.' etc.*

In the middle of all this is **Kirsten**. *She tries to reply, perhaps, to every tweet, every post, but it's all too much. She tries to switch off from it. Closing her laptop, switching off her phone, but more and more screens keep flickering on around her as the noise intensifies.*

11.

Petra, *with* **Derek**. **Derek** *has an arm around her. She has been crying.* **Kirsten** *arrives.*

Kirsten   Petra, for God's sake – I've been looking everywhere. Will you not answer your bloody phone? Petra? Petra, get in the car. There's something we need to talk about.

Derek   She's heard. Are you okay, love?

Kirsten   Don't call me that. Petra. It's okay. It'll be okay. She can't actually just force me out of a job, I mean – look I just need you to get into the car please.

Derek   Do as your mother says, Petra.

Kirsten   Keep out of this will you.

Petra   Everyone at school says you're mental.

Kirsten   Don't listen to them, it's just daft nonsense. It's your auntie being a – she's trying to undermine me. That's all. And it won't work. Because I'm right. So don't worry about that. Okay?

Petra   Someone called you a junkie.

Kirsten   What?

Petra   And someone else said you're a terrorist.

Kirsten   What? That's just kids being ridiculous love, that's just bullies making up nonsense. You have to credit their imaginations, I dunno what they'll come up with next –

Derek   Have you not read the article?

Kirsten   What article?

Petra *reads from her phone.*

Petra   'The Tragic Story of Provost Stockmann's Wayward Sister. After the surprise resignation of Kirsten Stockmann from the blah blah blah we look into the troubled past of this tragic figure and the unfortunate mistakes that led to her appointment.'

Kirsten   What the fuck.

Petra   'Her profound mental health difficulties.'

Kirsten   What?

Petra   'The drug-fuelled parties of her youth.'

Kirsten   I mean that's just parties, that's just student parties –

Petra   'Her criminal record and unlawful activities in London with known domestic extremists.'

Kirsten   I was a member of Greenpeace. It was a protest.

Petra   'Her promiscuous past and teenage pregnancy to tragic son of local businessman.'

Kirsten   Fucking hell Petra, I'm sorry –

Petra   Why are they doing this to us?

Kirsten   Who on Earth is publishing this nonsense?

Derek   Your pal.

Petra   Creepy McCreepface.

Kirsten   No, come on.

Derek   Fraid so. Benny Hovstad has written a hit piece on you Kirsten. Dunno what your sister's got on him but it must be bloody good.

Kirsten   Petra, get in the car.

Derek   I just want to say –

Kirsten   Get in the car Petra.

Derek   If I can just say – it's good what you're doing. Brave.
It takes chutzpah. So – you just keep at them. Okay? Just so you
stick it to them.

Kirsten   I thought you said it was all moonshine. Cockroaches.
A big laugh.

Derek   I believe you Kirsten. And, if the truth's on your side
then people will see that soon enough. So keep it up.

Kirsten   Why are you saying this?

Derek   Just trying to do my bit for, like, sticking up for the family.
That's all. And also, because, you know. I'm proud of you – of
your courage.

Kirsten   Okay. Well thank you.

Derek   In your piece you said it was – connected. To my, uh, my
land. Is that right? It's coming from my land? From the dump?

Kirsten   Fraid so.

Derek   Right.

Kirsten   Petra, let's go.

Derek   Well we'll see to that.

Kirsten   Petra, we're going.

Derek   Right. Okay. Right. We'll see to that.

12.

*A continuing cascade of social media posts and news clips. A Buzzfeed-style
reporter hounds a nervous **Aly** down the street. Online threats and abuse
directed at **Kirsten**, increasingly misogynistic and hateful in tone. Some of it
targets **Petra**, some of it threatens to dox them by posting their address. Other
conflicted voices of doubt, and fear. The online story escalating to national
news. Either onstage or onscreen we see **Kirsten** opening a door, being met
with a mob of paparazzi, slamming the door shut again. Everything arrives in*

a hurry, fragmented, bombarding. In and through this, **Aly**, *onstage, picks up a phone and calls someone.* **Benny** *answers.*

Benny   What?

Aly   I thought you said the water thing was a mistake? What's actually happening here?

Benny   The woman is deluded, okay, like I said. An error of judgement on my part –

Aly   It's all getting a bit out of hand is it no?

Benny   You know how much people want this thing to go ahead right?

Aly   Well aye, what do you think I've been doing all day? Some of the abuse she's getting is fucking brutal, like genuinely –

Benny   A bit spicy maybe. That's the internet for you –

Aly   I dunno –

Benny   Listen. You're an influential man Aly. You're well-loved around here, you know that. And if you want to start telling folk that you think Kirsten Stockmann has a point that's your prerogative alright? But see all that shite they're saying about her? You have to ask yourself whether you want that to be you. That's all.

Aly   What are you saying like?

Benny   We've all seen how easily the switch of public opinion can flip. And if you're not careful, it will eat you alive. Just think carefully mate, that's all I'm saying.

Aly   Look. Just tell me. Is the water safe or not?

Benny   Aye. The water's safe. As far as we know.

Aly   Right. Right, well that's fine then. That's fine.

Benny   See you in a couple of hours then. We're all looking forward to your DJ set!

The media onslaught continues. All the while **Kirsten**, *physically forcing her way through it all onstage, exhausted, until –*

13.

Kirsten *and* **Petra***'s house.* **Kirsten** *stares, stunned, a shell of a person. Silence.*

Petra   Right. Gimme your phone.

Kirsten   What?

Petra   Phone. Give it here.

Kirsten   What for like?

Petra   The guy from the campaign. Twitch guy. Popstar.

Kirsten   Aly? Ach, I wouldn't –

Petra   It's ringing.

Aly *watches his phone ring. Considers answering. Doesn't.* **Petra** *rings again.* **Aly** *picks up the phone this time, rejects the call.* **Petra** *puts the phone down.*

Kirsten   He's hung up hasn't he? He's hung up.

Petra   Voicemail. Wanker!

Kirsten*'s phone beeps.* **Petra** *looks at it.*

Petra   Why the fuck are you still getting Twitter notifications on this?

Kirsten   I don't know how to switch them off.

Petra   Right. I'm deleting your account.

Kirsten   What is it?

Petra   Nothing just –

Kirsten   What is Petra?

Petra   More of the same. Death threats. Rape threats. All the bantz.

Kirsten   I didn't want you to have to see that love –

Petra   Well, I don't want you to have to see it either, so – blip blap bloop. Deleted. Done.

Kirsten   I'm sorry.

Kirsten *starts to cry.*

Kirsten   I'm sorry. I've ruined it. I've ruined everything.

Petra   Mum. It's okay – you haven't! Please don't –

Kirsten   This was supposed to be it Petra, our big chance. I was trying to set us up in a place where we could be stable, secure.

Petra   Mum.

Kirsten   I'm sorry.

Silence.

Kirsten   We're really fucked now, Petra.

Pause.

Kirsten   My God what am I gonna do for money?

Pause.

Kirsten   I should just call Vonny now, tell her I'll write her statement and maybe –

Petra   Mum, stop it.

Kirsten   They are targeting *you* now Petra. I have to make this stop. I'll call Vonny and tell her I'll settle –

Petra   No! Mum! Fuck that. No. Did Chief Brody settle? Did he go 'okay then fine I'll just drop this'? When the Mayor refused to listen to him and refused to close the beaches even though they all knew there was a fucking shark out there, did Brody just shrug and go 'alright then, I suppose let's just *settle*'? Did he bollocks! He found a crazy old pirate and a fish scientist and went out to sea to catch that fucking shark like some kind of unstoppable Captain Ahab Moby Dick legend!

Kirsten   What the hell are you on about Petra?

Petra   Jaws. We watched it in Ms Quinn's Media Studies class. Only saw the first forty-five minutes, I'm guessing he catches the shark in the end right?

Kirsten   Yes. Yes he does.

Petra   See I knew it! I bet he swims out and kills that bastard shark with his own two hands!

Kirsten   That's actually exactly what he does, aye.

Petra   Well. There you go then. Do that.

Kirsten   I don't think I can sweetheart. I don't think I have it in me anymore.

Petra   Fine. I'll do it then.

Petra *leaves.* **Kirsten** *follows her.*

Kirsten   Petra. Petra!

14.

The space is transformed and we are in THE BIG SPLASH RESORT for the digital launch event. **Aly** *performs a beatbox and DJ set. It is sick! With him, co-hosting the launch event, is* **Vonny**, *with* **Benny** *also present. A boisterous live audience of townsfolk is joined by a much larger audience tuning in online. Their responses to events are visible throughout in the form of live text chat like on Twitch, Youtube, and Facebook Live broadcasts.*

Aly   Whoop whoop! Thank you! Thanks very much, you're all fantastic. More tunes coming up but first we've got a few speakers here to say a few words as we launch the good ship Big Splash on its maiden voyage. As most of you – all of you, probably uh, probably know, we've had to make a few last-minute changes to our line-up so – uh, consequently our first speaker this evening is the leader of our council the, woman who grabbed this whole project by the uh, the knackers and dragged it over the finish line, the formidable, the indomitable Vonny Stockman. Come on up here Vonny!

Enthusiasm in the chat for **Vonny**! *Emoji applause!*

Vonny   Thank you. Thanks very much.

She looks at her notes.

Vonny   Determination. Grit. Strength. Pride. These are the words I think of when I think about our town. And yet, when others speak about us, they often talk of these things as if in the past tense. 'A once-proud town' is a phrase we're all surely far too familiar with.

Vonny   The truth is we have always been proud of our community. But now – at last – we have something to show for it. A top-class facility, for top-class folk. Ensuring our people, our men, our women, our children can grow healthy, happy, and full of *life*. This is our brand new Big Splash –

Petra *bursts into the room, followed by* **Kirsten**.

Petra   Let Kirsten Stockmann speak!

Silence.

Petra   My mum is here and she'd like to say a few words –

Vonny   They are not supposed to be here!

Benny   Pull the broadcast Aly for fucksake!

Petra   Don't you fucking dare!

Aly *stands frozen. The broadcast runs on. Big WTF energy in the chat!*

Aly   Everyone, we have a – we have a bit of a strange one. There is a guest who –

Vonny   Aw Jesus.

Aly   Kirsten Stockmann, for you all watching at home, Kirsten was originally a scheduled speaker, and there has been a request to –

Vonny   Get them out of here! Get her out! This is ridiculous!

Petra   You're ridiculous!

Benny   She's not allowed here!

Aly   Can everyone. Just. Shut. The fuck! Up! For a minute!

Silence.

Aly   I think we should hear her out.

Vonny   You fucking wally.

Aly *mutes/unplugs* **Vonny***'s mic*

Vonny   This is outrageous!

Outrage in the chat! 'I heard she's a terrorist!' 'She's not a terrorist ya fanny!'
'Aye let her speak!' 'Chuck her out!' etc.

Aly   Kirsten will you come up here please.

Benny   Fucking hell.

Kirsten *approaches the stage/broadcast area. The chat goes wild!*

Kirsten*, shattered, rinsed, absolutely through the wringer, steps up to the mic.*
Silence. She stands, stoic and resolved. She appears to look every member of the
crowd and audience in the eye.

Kirsten   Hello. Contrary to what you might have been told, or
what you might have read or heard, I'm not deluded. All I've tried
to do from the start of this is to present you with the evidence.
The reality of how things are. I've taken the position that that's
the most respectful thing a person can do, simply presenting the
truth, however difficult or inconvenient or even nightmarish.
The honest truth.

And the truth is there is another sickness running through this
town, maybe even worse, even more harmful, than the poison in
our water. The horrible, sickening abuse my daughter and I have
been subject to today is repulsive enough on its own, but it's only
one symptom of an utterly sick society. A society that presents itself
as a fair and liberal democracy but in truth is built on nothing
other than outright lies, manipulation, and bullying. All at the
hands of our self-serving politicians, corrupt, destructive businesses,
and spineless, grovelling press.

Benny   Aly, get her mic out for God's sake!

Vonny   She can't just –

Aly   Everyone will you just shut it!

As **Kirsten** *speaks, the comments in the chat respond, increasingly fast, and wild.*

Kirsten   But you don't need me to tell you this. You know it
already, you're not idiots. We all know it don't we? Every one of you,
everybody here, everybody listening to this, knows about this sickness.
And yet it's almost as if we've come to accept it as some sort of
tolerable or even normal feature of who we are. A cancer that we've
decided to just live with, and somehow try to ignore. Like an ant that is
eaten alive from the inside out by some kind of parasite. We go about
our lives, wearing this outside appearance of a normal functioning
democracy. Pretending. When the truth is, on the inside, the body of it
all is diseased and rotten and putrid to the core. And we all know it.

Let me just say before I go on, that I really do have enormous
affection for this place, my home town. I was young when I left
and although my sister will tell you not to see me as one of your
own, I am. The years I spent away from here always felt like a kind
of exile if I'm totally honest. And it broke my heart. In the years
away, I developed a kind of rose-tinted nostalgia for this place, for
its people. Well, today has truly put paid to that.

See what I've discovered is that it's not the politicians, the press, or
the money men who are your real enemies here. No. It's *you*. It's
yourselves. The people of this town.

Aly   Aw come on you cannae be saying that –

Kirsten   This is the real discovery I've made today. You the
people. Complacently, idly believing whatever lie is told to you as
long as it makes you feel rewarded, and good about yourselves,
and comfortable. Day after day, decade after decade, lining up to
just let yourself be shafted from one generation to the next. These
people standing before you tonight were ready to let you die.

Vonny   Lies! Misinformation!

Kirsten   And for what? Short-term economic interests and
their own public image. And you were going to let them. Because
who actually wants to rework an entire infrastructure, an entire
plumbing system anyway? Sounds like a lot of hassle and expense

am I right? And for what? Better water? Better lives? A town we
can actually continue to live in? What's wrong with the water we've
got already, haven't they just told us just now that it's fine? In fact
we've heard it's good, we've heard it can't be made any better.
Toxic you say? Pour us another glass and we'll drink it right here.
I'm parched actually, give us another. Fill a bloody pool up and
we'll swim in the stuff. And here, aren't we lucky to even have a
pool in the first place? We were promised a pool. And we like the
promise! The promise is shiny and nice and best of all the promise
doesn't actually ask that we do anything or change anything! Why
rock the boat, right? Why risk trying to change things? Why make
a fuss? Why not just keep your head down and *choose* to just leave
it, and keep things as they are. All the while imagining that it was
never your responsibility in the first place. And so when things get
worse – and they will get worse – and when something needs to
be done, and the sickness simply cannot be ignored any longer,
you can tell yourselves all this is someone else's fault anyway. How
were you to know? You liked the promises you were made. You just
believed what they told you at the time. You were only going along
with what was said. And anyone who gets in the way, anyone who
does something so inconvenient as to point out the sickness that is
killing us, anyone who actually tries to do something about it, can
simply get fucked! Destroy her! Tear her down, and leave her lying
in the mud, the traitor! The witch! Crush her so completely she'll
never want to speak again! Well fuck you!

You – we – the people of this town have been brutally exploited
and abused and cast aside for generations by a system that hates us
and has always hated us. You don't need me to tell you that. But
Jesus Christ do you have to make it so fucking easy for them?

And that is the discovery I've made today. You, the people. You
cowards. You dickheads. You absolute shitebags. You're your own
worst enemy. And you always fucking have been.

Silence and stillness in the chat. Feedback from **Kirsten**'s *microphone. And
then, absolute fury!*

Vonny   There you have it! Kirsten Stockmann! An enemy of the
people!

Aly   Everyone just settle, okay, just settle down! We will not have threats in the chat, we will not –

Vonny   The people watching at home deserve to be heard, in their fullest! If they want to criticise and complain about what they've just seen then by God they have every right –

Kirsten *pushes her way past* **Vonny**, *making for the exit.* **Vonny** *pushes her back. They fight! Viciously, like little girls, like quarreling sisters.* **Petra** *grabs* **Kirsten** *and pulls her away.*

Benny   I warned you, I tried to warn you Kirsten –

Petra   Shut your fucking hole you pervy cunt.

Vonny, *bloody-nosed, reclaims the mic in the broadcast area.*

Vonny   Now we've all heard what she has to say! We can discount it, we can discount her and get back to – everyone – everyone quieten down! Please –

The chat is now just unhinged, on its own trajectory, outrage and fury. 'I know where she fucking lives' etc.

Vonny   Everyone! Everyone watching at home, everyone in the, in the chat – you are right to be angry! I am on your side, you are right to be angry but if you could please – we are going to press on. We are pressing ahead with – everyone! Please –

A deafening crash of NOISE as the ONLINE ANGER spilling out of the event becomes a cavalcade of VIOLENT MOB OUTRAGE. It is DIGITAL CARNAGE!

15.

Rubble, debris, broken glass. **Petra** *enters. She pours herself a bowl of cereal, and sits eating it, as she did the day before at the start of the play.*

Kirsten *enters, still in her clothes from the previous day, bin bag in hand. She surveys the scene in silence. She sets about picking up the mess, as* **Petra** *scrolls her phone. This continues for some time.* **Kirsten** *picks up a small rock. She holds it out to show* **Petra**.

Kirsten   Found another one.

Petra   Be finding a few more yet, I'd have thought.

Beat.

Petra   You know you've torn a big hole in the arse of your trousers as well, yeah?

Kirsten   Ah, shite! Twats.

Petra   You should never go out fighting for truth and justice in your best trousers, mum. Schoolgirl error.

Kirsten   Lesson learned.

Petra *starts playing a video on her phone. We can hear the audio from it. It is footage from last night, filmed on a phone camera.*

Kirsten   … You just believed what they told you at the time. You were only going along with what was said. When in fact, in the end, you've only got yourselves to blame for the absolute state of all of this, sickening sorry mess. That's the discovery I've made today. That you are your own worst enemy. You, the people. You cowards. You morons. You absolute shitebags. It's your fault, this mess. And it always fucking has been.

Kirsten   What are you doing?

Petra   Video. From last night. Someone's posted a clip. 'Mad Scientist Kirsten Stockmann makes discovery that we're all a massive pile of arseholes, basically.' Two hundred and eighty-six thousand views so far, apparently.

Kirsten   That's a lot.

Petra   Yeah, you're famous I guess. Yay. Listen to this: 'It is the opinion of this publication that Provost Vonny Stockmann deserves respect and praise for her resolve and determination in the face of the inevitable criticisms that will emerge, whatever comes to light in this impending review. The Provost has repeatedly insisted that the claims made by her sister lack veracity, but has nevertheless agreed to conduct an investigation. That alone should reassure everyone concerned that – '

Kirsten   Is this Benny?

Petra   Yup. Your bestie.

Kirsten   Fuck off.

Petra   Aaaand they've got an interview with Aunty Vonny, check it out.

Vonny   Of course we condemn in no uncertain terms the violence of last night, but we must also acknowledge the strength of feeling there is against those who would try to block the progress of this town.

Kirsten   Strength of feeling, Vonny? They smashed my fucking windows in.

Vonny   That strength of feeling is real, it is apparent all over social media, it's apparent in the streets, and we should listen to it. Yes, the opening of the Big Splash Resort will now be delayed – this is principally for minor repairs, and the accompanying review will undoubtedly put to rest any –

Petra *switches it off.*

Kirsten   Cow.

Petra   Still though. A review eh? That's something.

Kirsten *starts packing various things into cardboard boxes.* **Petra** *watches.*

Petra   Where we gonna go?

Kirsten   I dunno.

Petra   I mean, I don't think you're really gonna get much work round here now that you're the internet lady calling the people of the town every cunt under the sun.

Kirsten   Petra.

Petra   Just saying.

Beat.

Kirsten   London. We'll go back to London again, I don't know.

You can see your old pals again. That'll be nice.

Beat.

Petra   You weren't happy there. Were you?

Kirsten   No. No I wasn't.

Beat.

Kirsten   Australia then. This whole blasted rainy island can do one. Berlin. Somewhere European. That'd be nice.

Petra   How we gonna afford that?

Kirsten   Dunno. We're not.

Petra   And wouldn't you need a visa?

Kirsten   I haven't thought it through alright. I'm not good at this.

Beat.

Kirsten   I don't know what we'll do Petra. I'm sorry. But I don't.

They clean up together, **Kirsten** *unable to look at* **Petra***.*

A knock on the door. They look at each other.

Kirsten   I'll go.

Kirsten *exits, leaving* **Petra** *momentarily alone and nervous. She re-enters with* **Derek Kilmartin***.*

Petra   Grandad!

Derek   Hello sweetheart.

Derek *gives* **Petra** *a kiss on the head.*

Derek   Jings. A fine mess, this place. Still. Plenty of fresh air in through these windows, I'd have thought. So, every cloud.

Kirsten   Is there something in particular I can help you with or have you just come to take the piss?

Petra   Mum.

Derek   It's alright, it's alright. It's been a stressful time, for everyone. Here. Let me put the kettle on.

Derek *goes to the kettle. He goes to fill it up from the sink, then stops. He fills it up with bottled water, then flicks it on.*

Derek   Who wants tea? A good cup of tea will help yous feel better. And besides, I'm here with what I hope will be a bit of welcome good news.

Derek *plants a briefcase on the table.*

Derek   Anyone want to guess what's in this?

Petra   It's not another massive ice cream, is it?

Derek   Much better than that.

Derek *opens the briefcase, takes out a laptop, opens it on a screen displaying company shares.*

Petra   What's this?

Derek   These, Petra, are shares.

Kirsten   Shares?

Derek   Good old-fashioned shares. In the baths.

Kirsten   In the resort you mean?

Derek   They were not very difficult to get hold of today, I can tell you.

Kirsten   And you've bought –

Derek   As many as I could possibly pay for, aye. In fact, you are both standing in the company of the new *majority shareholder*. Which sort of makes me the boss of the place.

Petra   Ha ha, what the fuck.

Kirsten   What on Earth have you gone and done that for? You're aware of the state of the place's reputation, those shares are utterly worthless –

Derek   Well, they were certainly available on the cheap aye, let's say that much. Folk couldn't get out of there quick enough.

Kirsten   So what are you playing at? I don't get it.

Derek   The reputation of the place Kirsten, is something you'll be able to help me turn around. If you're a good girl.

Kirsten   A good girl.

Petra   Grandad, ew.

Derek   You'd said in the wee piece that you put on the internet that the source of this – pollution shall we call it – was related to the, eh, the business activities taking place on my land, is that right?

Kirsten   That's right. And you said you'd sort it.

Derek   Exactly. And that's what we'll do. See, I couldn't sit silent on something like that, could I? I know I'm not a well-liked man around here, Kirsten. But I've always put that down to jealousy, as opposed to any actual harm I might have caused anyone. I've always taken good care of my image. These allegations – they're not great for me. It's dirty. It's a bad dirty look, and at the end of the day it's bad for business. I've lived in this town my whole life. I've built what I have from nothing. And I intend to go out a clean man, Kirsten, with a clean reputation.

Kirsten   Well I'm afraid you've shat the bed a bit with that one Derek –

Derek   I don't think so. See that's where you come in. Like a holiday visit to a state-of-the-art spa resort, you are going to *cleanse* me, Kirsten.

Kirsten   Is that right aye.

Derek   The shares as I said, were easy enough to get hold off. But it's still tricky to pull together the capital in such a short time you know. It's all tied up in this, that, or the other. So do you know what money I bought these shares with? No, of course you don't. There was this wee side fund I had for money that was gonna go to Petra after I'm gone –

Petra   Grandad, what?

Derek   Ach, your mum wanted me to tell you about it, what with the way things have been. And I don't think you knew quite how much was in there did you Kirsten? Or *was* in there, rather. Now it's here. Wrapped up in these, as you say, utterly worthless shares.

Petra   Grandad what the fuck?

Derek   Don't worry sweetheart, I promised you both didn't I, that I would support you. And I will. All you have to do is retract this moonshine you've been putting out about my land.

Derek *takes a bunch of papers out of the briefcase.*

Derek   My lawyers have it all written up but you can add some of your own creative flair, within reason. Of course there is also some paperwork to make sure you don't go off the rails again – I don't like to use the phrase 'gagging order' but you get the gist. We shake hands, our reputations are slowly restored. We let this business with your sister and the water run its course, you get your job back in time, when things have died down. And we run a successful wee family venture together in relative comfort. Or the alternative is, the opposite. The absolute opposite of that for you both, on every count.

The kettle clicks off.

Derek   Who wanted tea? I won't bother if it's just myself. Come on, let's have a cup of tea to celebrate.

Petra   Grandad, I can't fucking believe you!

Derek   Aye, kids can be fiery about these things. And you were fiery too when you were Petra's age, Kirsten! But it's fair to say that's got you into a bit of bother over the years hasn't it? And as grown adults – no disrespect now Petra – we understand how the world works. We know what principles *really* are. And what greater principle is there, than looking after the long-term wellbeing of your own family, your own daughter? You'd be crazy, absolutely barking mad, not to. So now we get to find out if you actually are a principled woman Kirsten. Or if you really are just a fucking heidcase after all.

Petra   Mum, say something, tell him.

Derek   No, no, Don't worry. Take some time to think it over. It always feels better that way. I'll call in on you again later. Here, I'll leave this pen though, just in case you can't find one. Tattie bye.

Derek *exits.*

Petra   Mum.

Beat.

Petra   Mum, you're not actually thinking of −

Kirsten   I don't know what I should do Petra, I don't −

Petra   If you say yes to that I will never look at you in the same way again.

Beat.

Petra   And not like, in a good way. I mean like in a bad way, obviously. The bad one of that.

Beat.

Petra   You can't agree to this mum. I won't let you.

Kirsten   Just − just keep packing up for now, and −

Petra   Mum.

Kirsten   Aye?

Petra   I don't actually really want to keep moving all the time.

Kirsten   Okay. So I sign the paper and we do what he says −

Petra   No, I mean. I don't want to move. But I don't want to do that either.

Kirsten   You can't mean staying here like this love, surely?

Petra *shrugs.*

Petra   I don't think we should let them push us around. I don't think we should have to go because they don't like us. And I don't think you should have to lie for us to stay. You said this place is my home. Our home. And maybe it is. That's what I think. I think we should stay. And fuck 'em.

Petra   Stay, and be right. And keep saying what's right. And keep staying. And rinse and repeat and, well, we'll be proved right eventually. Probably. Maybe. And then they'll all just have to catch up. And then they'll be sorry. And even if they're not – well –

Kirsten   I don't know, Petra.

Petra   We've already won, really. They just don't know it yet.

Kirsten   It's difficult, Petra. It's difficult being so alone –

Petra   We'll be alright. We've got each other.

Pause. **Petra** *hands her the legal paperwork.*

Petra   Here. Tear it. Tear it up.

Kirsten   Oh, Petra I don't know –

Petra   Yes you do. You do. Tear it.

Kirsten *takes the paper. Thinks. Then rips it.*

Petra   Yes!

Petra *grabs some paper and tears it too. They scrunch it up and tear it into confetti and throw it around and stamp on it, laughing.*

Petra   Shove it up your arse! Shove it up your arse!

Kirsten   Fucking hell Petra. Oh God –

The paperwork thoroughly pulverised, they stop.

Petra   Well that's that answered then.

Kirsten   Petra?

Petra   Mm?

Kirsten   You really are a wee terror you know that? You're a total riot.

Petra   Yeah. I got that from someone I think. Gimme a bag. Let's just keep cleaning up.

They clean up the mess together, picking up pieces of rubble and of torn paper and depositing each in bin bags. It takes a long time. As they work together, the shared giddy excitement fades. An uncertainty falls on **Kirsten** *as she watches her daughter, full of rebellious optimism, preparing for a future that will undoubtedly hurt her. Has she done the right thing? Will she change her mind? As they continue tidying, they are together, but very apart, as the reality of their uncertain future unfolds in the mess of this life. They continue cleaning, in silence, as the lights fade out.*

End of Play.

Methuen Drama Modern Plays
include work by

Bola Agbaje
Edward Albee
Davey Anderson
Jean Anouilh
John Arden
Peter Barnes
Sebastian Barry
Alistair Beaton
Brendan Behan
Edward Bond
William Boyd
Bertolt Brecht
Howard Brenton
Amelia Bullmore
Anthony Burgess
Leo Butler
Jim Cartwright
Lolita Chakrabarti
Caryl Churchill
Lucinda Coxon
Curious Directive
Nick Darke
Shelagh Delaney
Ishy Din
Claire Dowie
David Edgar
David Eldridge
Dario Fo
Michael Frayn
John Godber
Paul Godfrey
James Graham
David Greig
John Guare
Mark Haddon
Peter Handke
David Harrower
Jonathan Harvey
Iain Heggie

Robert Holman
Caroline Horton
Terry Johnson
Sarah Kane
Barrie Keeffe
Doug Lucie
Anders Lustgarten
David Mamet
Patrick Marber
Martin McDonagh
Arthur Miller
D. C. Moore
Tom Murphy
Phyllis Nagy
Anthony Neilson
Peter Nichols
Joe Orton
Joe Penhall
Luigi Pirandello
Stephen Poliakoff
Lucy Prebble
Peter Quilter
Mark Ravenhill
Philip Ridley
Willy Russell
Jean-Paul Sartre
Sam Shepard
Martin Sherman
Wole Soyinka
Simon Stephens
Peter Straughan
Kate Tempest
Theatre Workshop
Judy Upton
Timberlake Wertenbaker
Roy Williams
Snoo Wilson
Frances Ya-Chu Cowhig
Benjamin Zephaniah

For a complete listing of
Methuen Drama titles, visit:

www.bloomsbury.com/drama

Follow us on Twitter and keep up to date
with our news and publications

@MethuenDrama

Methuen Drama Contemporary Dramatists

include

John Arden (two volumes)
Arden & D'Arcy
Peter Barnes (three volumes)
Sebastian Barry
Mike Bartlett
Dermot Bolger
Edward Bond (ten volumes)
Howard Brenton (two volumes)
Leo Butler (two volumes)
Richard Cameron
Jim Cartwright
Caryl Churchill (two volumes)
Complicite
Sarah Daniels (two volumes)
Nick Darke
David Edgar (three volumes)
David Eldridge (two volumes)
Ben Elton
Per Olov Enquist
Dario Fo (two volumes)
Michael Frayn (four volumes)
John Godber (four volumes)
Paul Godfrey
James Graham (two volumes)
David Greig
John Guare
Lee Hall (two volumes)
Katori Hall
Peter Handke
Jonathan Harvey (two volumes)
Iain Heggie
Israel Horovitz
Declan Hughes
Terry Johnson (three volumes)
Sarah Kane
Barrie Keeffe
Bernard-Marie Koltès (two volumes)
Franz Xaver Kroetz
Kwame Kwei-Armah
David Lan
Bryony Lavery
Deborah Levy
Doug Lucie

David Mamet (four volumes)
Patrick Marber
Martin McDonagh
Duncan McLean
David Mercer (two volumes)
Anthony Minghella (two volumes)
Tom Murphy (six volumes)
Phyllis Nagy
Anthony Neilson (two volumes)
Peter Nichol (two volumes)
Philip Osment
Gary Owen
Louise Page
Stewart Parker (two volumes)
Joe Penhall (two volumes)
Stephen Poliakoff (three volumes)
David Rabe (two volumes)
Mark Ravenhill (three volumes)
Christina Reid
Philip Ridley (two volumes)
Willy Russell
Eric-Emmanuel Schmitt
Ntozake Shange
Sam Shepard (two volumes)
Martin Sherman (two volumes)
Christopher Shinn (two volumes)
Joshua Sobel
Wole Soyinka (two volumes)
Simon Stephens (three volumes)
Shelagh Stephenson
David Storey (three volumes)
C. P. Taylor
Sue Townsend
Judy Upton
Michel Vinaver (two volumes)
Arnold Wesker (two volumes)
Peter Whelan
Michael Wilcox
Roy Williams (four volumes)
David Williamson
Snoo Wilson (two volumes)
David Wood (two volumes)
Victoria Wood